GRANT HILL

BASKETBALL'S HIGH FLIER

BY BILL GUTMAN

MILLBROOK SPORTS WORLD
THE MILLBROOK PRESS
BROOKFIELD, CONNECTICUT

Photographs courtesy of NBA Photos: cover (Nathaniel S. Butler), cover inset (Andrew Bernstein), p. 15 (Jen Pottheiser); Duke University: pp. 3 (photo by Michael B. Hirsch), 13; Allsport: pp. 4 (J. Patronite), 17, 19 (Earl Richardson), 22-23 (Jonathan Daniel), 24 (Jonathan Daniel), 30 (Doug Pensinger), 31 (Doug Pensinger), 39 (Jonathan Daniel), 44 (Jonathan Daniel), 46; Wide World Photos: pp. 8, 42; NFL Photos: p. 10; © 1992, 1994 Bob Donnan Photography: pp. 26, 28, 35; Bettmann: pp. 33, 37; Focus on Sports: p. 40.

Library of Congress Cataloging-in-Publication Data
Gutman, Bill.
Grant Hill : basketball's high flier / by Bill Gutman.
p. cm. — (Millbrook sports world)
Includes bibliographical references and index.
Summary: Covers the basketball career of the forward for the Detroit Pistons who was also a star player at Duke University.
ISBN 0-7613-0038-4 (lib. bdg.)

1. Hill, Grant—Juvenile literature. 2. Basketball players—United States—Biography—Juvenile literature. [1. Hill, Grant. 2. Basketball players. 3. Afro-Americans—Biography.] I. Title. II. Series.
GV884.H55G88 1996
796.323'092—dc20 [B] 96-6421 CIP AC

Published by The Millbrook Press, Inc.
2 Old New Milford Road
Brookfield, Connecticut 06804

GRANT HILL

On March 28, 1992, the Blue Devils of Duke University and the Wildcats of the University of Kentucky stepped onto the court at the Spectrum in Philadelphia for one of the biggest college basketball games of the year. It was the East Regional Final of the NCAA Tournament. The winner would go to the fabled Final Four with a chance to win the national championship.

Duke came in as the favorite. The Blue Devils had lost just two games all year and were ranked number one in the country. In addition, they were

Grant Hill was a complete player right from the beginning of his career at Duke. Here he dribbles around a defender in a game against Arizona.

the defending national champion with a chance to make it two straight. But Kentucky had a high-scoring team that liked to press on defense and take a lot of three-point shots.

Led by the flawless shooting of star center Christian Laettner, Duke took a 50-45 lead at the half. When the lead got to double digits early in the second half, it looked as if Duke would win going away. Then Kentucky's Jamal Mashburn led a Wildcat comeback that closed the gap. At the end of regulation time, the score was tied at 93 in one of the most exciting college games of the year.

Mashburn had fouled out, but John Pelphrey of Kentucky opened the overtime period by hitting a long three-pointer. Seconds later, Duke's Bobby Hurley answered with a three of his own. The two teams continued to battle. With time winding down, Duke had a 102-101 lead but Kentucky had the ball. Guard Sean Wood drove across the key and put up a double-pumper. It went in, giving Kentucky a 103-102 lead. Duke called timeout with just 2.1 seconds left.

The Blue Devils were in trouble. They had to take the ball out under their own basket. If they simply threw it into their backcourt they would only have time for a long desperation heave. They had to try a long pass down into the frontcourt. It was a gamble, but Duke Coach Mike Krzyzewski (pronounced: sha-shef-ski) diagrammed a play, then quietly told his team, "We're going to get a good shot. We can win."

The coach sent Laettner to stand in front of the foul line with his back to the basket. The big guy hadn't missed a shot throughout the entire game. Two Kentucky players set up behind him, but no one was in front of him. Coach K's choice to put the ball in bounds was his sensational sophomore forward, Grant Hill.

Hill was a remarkably talented, 6-foot-8 (203-centimeter) player who could do everything on the court. He already had 11 points and 10 rebounds against Kentucky, but now he was being called upon to deliver the biggest pass of his basketball life.

Looking quickly downcourt, Hill saw that there still was no defender in front of Laettner. Without hesitation he wound up and fired a pass that traveled more than 75 feet (23 meters) in a straight line. It was a pass that would have made a professional football quarterback proud. It hit Laettner right in the hands. Laettner knew he had precious little time. He faked to right, then turned left and fired up a fallaway jumper just before the buzzer sounded.

The ball floated in the air, then swished through the net! Duke had won the game on Laettner's miracle shot, 104-103. The team was again going to the Final Four. With his 31st point, Laettner was the big hero. Almost forgotten in the wild scene that followed was Grant Hill's long pass. Had it been even slightly off the mark, Laettner might not have had time to fake and shoot.

But Hill wasn't looking for credit. He had simply done the job he was given, and the team had won. That was always the important thing. Grant Hill had always been a team player, and this trait had enabled him to become one of the best in the game.

CHILDHOOD VALUES

Begin with a father who graduated from Yale University with a history major and was a star running back for the Dallas Cowboys. Add a mother who graduated from Wellesley College and became a practicing attorney. Chances are that their son would have a jump-start on life. This was the case with Grant Henry Hill.

Grant was born in Dallas, Texas, on October 5, 1972. That year his father, Calvin Hill, was en route to gaining 1,036 yards as a 6-foot-4 (193-centimeter), 230-pound (104-kilogram) running back with the Cowboys. The elder Hill had gone from Yale to become National Football League Rookie of the Year in 1969. He was also wearing a Super Bowl ring that he and his Dallas teammates had won in January 1972.

At 15 months, little Grant was photographed enjoying a quiet moment with his parents, Janet and Calvin Hill. Calvin was recovering from a dislocated elbow, an injury he received as a star running back for the Dallas Cowboys.

By the time Grant was born, his mother, Janet, had graduated from Wellesley where she was a suitemate of Hillary Rodham, who would become the wife of President Bill Clinton and First Lady of the country. After giving birth to Grant, Janet Hill continued her education, eventually becoming an attorney.

Grant was an only child. His mother and father also were only children, so there was no extended family, no brothers and sisters, no uncles and aunts. His mother and father were achievers, working hard to learn and make things happen. They wanted their son to have a rich and varied educational background. That way, he would be able to make his own choices. And perhaps he would have the same work ethic and desire to achieve that they did.

By 1978, after Calvin Hill had retired from football, the family moved to Reston, Virginia. Janet began working as an attorney in nearby Washington, D.C., and Calvin soon joined the Baltimore Orioles baseball team as one of the first black executives in professional sports.

The Hills became involved with their young son's education, trying to make it as well rounded as possible. Grant began studying piano at almost the same time he began school. In addition, he traveled the world with his parents, to places like Egypt and England, meeting all kinds of people.

His fun also included sports. But when young Grant began showing a real interest in sports, his father expressed concern about another possible problem.

"I never anticipated that I'd have a son who would turn out to be a great athlete," Calvin Hill said. "I even thought that someday I might have to help him work his way through an identity crisis when he realized he'd never be as good as Dad."

But Grant was a levelheaded kid. He says now that he never felt any pressure to be another Calvin Hill.

Calvin Hill had been a slashing runner for the Cowboys, good enough to be Rookie of the Year and become a 1000-yard rusher.

"I always felt I had an advantage as a result of having a father who was an athlete and growing up in a sports atmosphere," he said. "He [Calvin] was always available to help me. But I never felt any pressure to follow in his footsteps."

Soccer and basketball were the first sports that Grant played. He always said that soccer gave him the coordination and fluid movement that helped him excel at basketball. But the sport he didn't play was football—his parents wouldn't permit it. They felt that he was too young and didn't want him to risk getting a serious injury.

When Grant was in the eighth grade at Langston Hughes Junior High in Reston, his father came to speak at the school. Grant was so embarrassed that he faked an illness and stayed in the nurse's office. Another time, his father picked him up in a Porsche after basketball practice. Grant asked him to please drive the family's other car, a Volkswagen, the next time he came. Because his family was financially secure and could enjoy many luxuries, Grant felt self-conscious around other kids his age, many of whom didn't have as much.

"I just didn't want to appear better than others," he said.

Grant did well in his studies and in sports in elementary school and then in middle school, but showed no sign that sports would become more than just a hobby. And his parents never pushed him.

"It didn't matter to us if Grant had chosen to pursue, say, art or music instead of sports," Calvin Hill said. "As long as he gave it his best effort."

THE ROAD TO STARDOM

By the eighth grade at Langston Hughes Junior High, it was apparent that basketball was Grant's best sport. He played on an AAU (Amateur Athletic Union) team that won the championship of the 13-and-under age group. Grant was already about 6 feet 2 (188 centimeters) and growing fast. He was quick, a fine jumper and rebounder, a good ballhandler and shooter, and was developing an all-around game.

Being an athlete all his life, Calvin Hill enjoyed backyard games with his son. "We played whatever sport was in season," the elder Hill recalled. "And I usually held back a little so I wouldn't hurt his [Grant's] confidence."

After Grant returned from his AAU experience, his father challenged him to a backyard game of one-on-one. As usual, Calvin held back a bit, and before he knew it, Grant beat him. They played again. This time the former Dallas Cowboy played as hard as he could, but his son won again. At the age of 13, Grant was becoming an outstanding player.

When most of his friends were ninth graders in their freshman year at South Lakes High School, Grant was still at Langston Hughes Junior High, looking forward to the next year when he could play alongside them on the junior varsity team.

But when Grant tried out for the team, Coach Wendell Byrd felt that he should skip junior varsity competition and join the varsity immediately. Grant was already a better player for his age than most. Joining the varsity, he quickly became a starter as a freshman during the 1986-1987 season. A year later, as a 15-year-old sophomore, he averaged 25 points a game for South Lakes High. He was off and running.

Grant continued to be aware of his background. He knew he had certain advantages that other kids did not. But eventually he turned that into a positive for him. As his father said, "What motivates Grant is to show that his success has nothing to do with what he is given and everything to do with what he earns."

In his final two years at South Lakes High he earned nothing but praise. Grant was already taller than his father and still growing. He could control a high school game with his all-around skills — passing, scoring, and rebounding. He had become a dominant player, a prep superstar who appeared to have a big future in the game.

Nothing he did dispelled that notion. Grant kept getting better. South Lakes won the state championship in both those years. And by the time he was a senior, Grant was averaging 29 points a game, as well as 11 rebounds and 8 assists. Not surprisingly, he was a prep All-American as well as an outstanding student. He was nearly at his full height of 6 feet 8 inches (203 centimeters) and weighed more than 200 pounds (90 kilograms).

With his background, academic standing, and basketball talent, he could have his pick of just about any college.

BLUE DEVILS SENSATION

Grant Hill graduated from South Lakes High in June 1990. He was not yet 18 years old. Now he had to make one of the biggest decisions of his life — picking a college. Many thought that he would choose Georgetown, in Washington, D.C., whose basketball team he had followed since 1982. But he also had North Carolina on his list, as well as Virginia, Michigan, and Duke. All five had outstanding basketball programs, as well as solid academic reputations. And all wanted Grant Hill.

But in the end, the decision wasn't difficult. All it took was one visit to the Duke University campus in Durham, North Carolina.

"I made my first official visit to Duke and decided on the spot that it was a perfect fit," Grant said. "I liked its size, its atmosphere and Coach [Mike] Krzyzewski's honesty. His system provided players with a lot of freedom on offense, and they didn't seem scared to make mistakes. I felt it would showcase my strengths."

One visit to Duke University in Durham, North Carolina, convinced Grant that this was the college for him. He enrolled as a freshman in the fall of 1990 and looked comfortable on the campus from the first.

Grant made no other campus visits and in the fall of 1990 began his freshman year at Duke. He was now officially a Blue Devil.

The Duke program had always been highly successful. In 1989-1990, the season before Grant arrived, the team made it to the final game of the National Collegiate Athletic Association (NCAA) Tournament to determine the national champion. There, they were blown out by an explosive University of Nevada at Las Vegas (UNLV) team, 103-73.

The two returning Duke stars for the 1990-1991 season were 6-foot-11 (210-centimeter) junior center Christian Laettner and 6-foot (183-centimeter) sophomore point guard Bobby Hurley. Both were considered possible All-Americans. The other starters were senior Greg Koubek at forward and sophomore Thomas Hill at guard. The fifth starting spot was still open.

Once Coach K and his staff saw Grant Hill in action they knew he was the man for the job. Though he had just turned 18, Grant was already poised and remarkably athletic. He could handle the ball like a guard and was an outstanding leaper and a fine defensive player. But perhaps his biggest asset was that he always thought of the team first. He didn't worry about his own numbers: Winning the game was the most important thing.

The Blue Devils were off to a fast start, winning five of their first six games. Grant contributed right away. He became the first Duke freshman since Johnny Dawkins to score in double figures in his first six career games. He had fit in with the team like a glove. Grant was well liked by his teammates and a popular figure on the Duke campus.

Grant's career at Duke University got off to a flying start and stayed that way. In his first six games he scored in the double figures.

Besides starring on the basketball team, Grant earned good grades from the beginning. He had found a balance between athletics and academics. Now he wanted to help his team win as many games as they could.

NATIONAL CHAMPIONS TWICE

The Blue Devils were proving to be an outstanding basketball team. They were ranked in the top ten for a good part of the season, with a number of big wins. They also led the tough Atlantic Coast Conference (ACC).

Grant continued to play well. He scored a season-high 19 points three times — against Michigan, Oklahoma, and Arizona. But more important, he did whatever it took to help his team win. He would be just as satisfied making a pass or grabbing a rebound as he would scoring points. Sometimes he concentrated more on defense, shutting down a top opponent. Whatever he did, it was the best.

A broken nose suffered in January caused him to miss a few games and to not start in several others. But there was little doubt that even as a freshman, Grant had become an important part of a top team. The Blue Devils finished the regular season with a 25-6 record and were first in the ACC. They were also ranked number six in the country by both the Associated Press (AP) and United Press International (UPI). The number one team in the country was undefeated Nevada-Las Vegas. The Runnin' Rebels were heavy favorites to repeat as NCAA champs.

Now came the all-important postseason. First was the ACC tournament. Duke was the favorite, but was upset by North Carolina, 96-74, in the second round of the championship tournament. With four underclassmen, including a freshman and two sophomores, in the starting lineup, maybe the Blue Devils weren't quite ready for prime time.

The team then became the number two seed in the Midwest Region as the NCAA Tournament began. They ripped through the region, finally whipping an excellent St. John's team, 78-61, in the regional final.

Now the Blue Devils were going to the Final Four for the fourth straight year. But standing in their way in the semifinals was UNLV. Led by all-Americans Larry Johnson and Stacey Augmon, the Rebels were a powerhouse who had been dominating opponents all year. In fact, the unbeaten Rebels had won 45 straight games.

Before the game began at the Hoosier Dome in Indianapolis, Coach K told his team that they could win by challenging the Rebels and playing aggressively at both ends of the court. With Grant scoring the first two points and Laettner playing a brilliant game, the Blue Devils jumped out to an early lead, though UNLV had come back to take a slim 43-41 advantage at halftime.

Grant cuts down the net in celebration of a win during the 1991 season.

It stayed close throughout the second half. The Rebels tried to widen their lead, but the poised Blue Devils refused to crack. UNLV held a 74-71 lead with 3:51 left. Seconds later, Anderson Hunt made a layup to increase the UNLV lead to 76-71. It didn't look good for the Blue Devils.

But Duke hung tough. Bobby Hurley and Thomas Hill each connected on clutch three-pointers. With the clock running down, the game was tied at 77-77. Laettner got the ball with 12 seconds left and was fouled. He made both free throws to give the Blue Devils a 79-77 lead. Then Duke's defense took over. Hunt's three-point try at the buzzer clanged off the rim. Duke had won it and was in the final. And it had beaten a team that many had considered unbeatable.

Laettner led the way with 28 points. Brian Davis scored 15 off the bench, while Bobby Hurley had 12. Grant scored 11 points, making five of eight shots from the floor and one for one from the line. He also was second to Laettner with five rebounds and second to Hurley with five assists. He had played a fine, all-around game.

Now the Blue Devils would face Kansas for the national championship. This one was a little easier. The first time Duke got the ball Hurley snapped a long, line drive pass toward the basket. Suddenly Grant leaped high above everyone, grabbed the ball with one hand and slammed it home with ferocity. His opening hoop set the tone for the game.

A confident Duke team took a 42-34 lead at the half, then cruised home to win its first national title with a 72-65 victory. Laettner again led the way

Against Kansas for the championship, Grant showed his all-around floor game as Duke won the national title. Here he goes airborne, staying in control before hitting a teammate with a pass.

with 18 points. Grant had just 10, but only took six shots from the floor. His eight rebounds and three assists once again showcased his versatility.

For the season, Grant averaged 11.2 points, grabbed 183 rebounds for a 5.1 average, and had 79 assists. He made the Atlantic Coast Conference All-Freshman team and was also named a freshman All-American. He couldn't ask for much more, and neither could his father.

"Winning the Super Bowl was a tremendous high for me," Calvin Hill said. "But it was no match for the feeling I had when I left the Hoosier Dome after Duke won the title last year."

With four starters back and Brian Davis replacing Greg Koubek, the Blue Devils were even better in 1991-1992. This time Duke ripped through the regular season. The team won its first 17 games and finished with a 25-2 record to be ranked the number one team in the country. Now it was time to defend its national title.

Respect for Grant had grown throughout the year. At one point Hurley missed five straight games with an injury. In a surprise move, Coach K moved Grant into the important point guard position. Grant performed beautifully without missing a beat. He handled the ball, ran the offense, and kept the team on a winning note.

Grant admitted he enjoyed the temporary change of positions. "Christian [Laettner] was on his way to becoming Player of the Year," explained Grant afterward. "And I could control whether he got the ball. That was a power thing for me, and it was kind of nice."

In the postseason, the Blue Devils easily won the ACC Tournament, topping North Carolina by 20 points in the final, 94-74. In that game, Grant hit all eight shots from the field and scored 20 points.

Duke entered the NCAA tourney as the number one seed in the East Regional. There they topped Campbell, Iowa, and Seton Hall to set up their memorable regional final against Kentucky. In that game Grant made the long pass to Laettner in the final seconds of overtime to allow Duke a return trip to the Final Four. It was the fifth straight year the Blue Devils had been there.

In the semifinal, Duke had to battle Bobby Knight's Indiana Hoosiers. It was a hard-fought game with the Blue Devils finally winning, 81-78. Hurley led the way with 26 points, followed by Grant with 14. Now the team would be defending its championship against Michigan. The Wolverines had five freshman starters led by Chris Webber and Jalen Rose. Known as the Fab Five, the Michigan team had captured the fancy of the basketball world.

With starting forward Brian Davis slowed by a bad ankle sprain and Laettner getting off to a terrible start, the Blue Devils looked sluggish. But Michigan was missing key shots as well, and the game was close for the entire first half. At the break the Wolverines had a one-point lead, 31-30.

It was apparent that the Duke players were tired. The game remained close until midway through the second half. Then Laettner and Grant began to make big plays. In fact, Grant electrified the crowd several times with brilliant baseline drives to the hoop. He also helped the team to control the boards on the defensive end.

In the final minutes, Duke pulled away to win, 71-51, repeating as national champions. Laettner wound up with 19 points, followed by Grant with 18. Grant also led the club with 10 rebounds and had 5 assists, second to Hurley's seven. He had played a superb game. But he had been doing that in NCAA tournaments for two years.

"Christian and Bobby were the MVP's [of the 1991 and 1992 Final Fours]," said Coach Krzyzewski, "but the guy who played as well as anybody in those four games was Grant."

For the year, Grant averaged 14 points a game, shooting 61.1 percent from the field. He also had 187 rebounds and 134 assists. He was a second-

team All-America selection by the UPI and was awarded an honorable mention All-America by the AP. He had become an outstanding ballplayer. In fact, many felt he was already good enough to play in the National Basketball Association (NBA).

THE MEANING OF COMMITMENT

More and more collegiate underclassman were joining the NBA. Some were leaving school after their sophomore year and getting multi-million dollar contracts from the pros. With Christian Laettner and Brian Davis having graduated, it was doubtful the Blue Devils would win a third straight title. But with Bobby Hurley, Thomas Hill, and the young Cherokee Parks and Antonio Lang, the team would still be solid. Especially if Grant Hill returned.

Grant wasted little time in letting everyone know his intentions. "One thing my mom always taught me was to honor my commitments," he said, shortly after returning to Duke

Grant (33) and his teammates help Coach Krzyzewski celebrate a second straight national championship in 1992.

Although the temptation must have been great to turn pro after his junior year, Grant felt he had made a commitment to Duke for the full four years. Here he relaxes with his teammates on the bench.

in the fall of 1992 for his junior year. "I made a commitment to Coach K and the school that I would be here for four years, and he made a commitment to me that he would coach me for four years."

So Grant was back. Before basketball began, he plunged back into his studies. He was a history major and always kept his grades up, balancing classwork and basketball. In a big-time basketball program, this is difficult to do. But a high percentage of the Duke ballplayers were good students who graduated with their class.

Grant was also becoming more active in other ways. He would often speak to kids about the value of staying in school and working toward goals. One of his main interests was Summit III: Preparing Our Sons for Manhood, a program that sought to encourage young African Americans to develop positive habits and self-esteem.

Among the things he stressed to his school-age audiences was that "academics is more important than athletics" because "very few people make it to the pros." Also important were setting goals, both long and short term, and respect for one's parents. "They love you, they care for you and they've been on this earth longer, so they know what's going on."

In addition, he talked about the importance of personal integrity. His example was his commitment to Duke for four years. He also spoke about the dangers of drugs and alcohol.

"I've gone through 20 years and have never tried any drugs or any alcohol," he said. "Today it seems that kids are starting to drink at a much younger age. Kids need to realize that they can have fun without getting involved with that stuff."

He also talked about athletes as role models, a topic discussed often. What responsibility do big-time athletes have as role models? Some feel they shouldn't have any. Others feel they should. Here's what Grant Hill said: "I think it's unfortunate in today's society that people look up to entertainers and athletes the way they do, as opposed to a parent or someone who's real. I did the same thing when I was growing up.

"A lot of times we are placed — and I guess I'm in that category — into situations where we are role models. So we have that responsibility to not let [people] down. If what I say affects one person, if only one person listens and takes something from that and applies it to himself, I've been successful."

So even though he was just a junior in college, Grant already felt he had a responsibility as a star athlete. On the court, Grant was better than ever. But, as expected, the team wasn't quite the force of two years before. They won their first ten games, but after that ran into some problems, especially against the tough ACC foes.

Duke finished the regular season at 23-6. Then in the ACC tournament they were beaten by Georgia Tech, 69-66. And in the NCAA tourney the Blue Devils whipped Southern Illinois, 105-70, before losing in the second

The worst thing for a basketball player is not being able to play. Grant missed six games because of a sprained toe during the 1992-1993 season. Even though the Blue Devils didn't win another championship, Grant was named college basketball's Defensive Player of the Year.

round to California, 82-77. So Duke was done for the year, finishing at 24-8.

But Grant had earned even more respect. He was a second-team UPI All-America selection and was named to the third team by the AP. Better yet, the nation's coaches named him, as the country's top defensive player, the recipient of the Henry Iba Corinthian Award. That was a high honor. For the year he averaged 18 points a game, despite missing six games with a sprained toe. He also averaged a career best 6.4 rebounds and led the team with 64 steals.

Now he had one more year at Duke. True to his word, he returned to fulfill the remainder of his commitment.

CONSENSUS ALL-AMERICAN

Bobby Hurley and Thomas Hill graduated after the 1992-1993 season. Now Grant was the only remaining starter from the two championship teams.

"I want to give [my new teammates] memories, like the ones I have from playing with Bobby [Hurley], Christian [Laettner], and Brian [Davis]."

Coach Krzyzewski wasn't surprised by Grant's positive attitude. "What's great about Grant," he said, "especially for somebody as good as he is, is that he's always aware of other people's feelings. And he has great empathy for other people."

Grant took the court for his fourth and final season as a Blue Devil. He was joined in the starting unit by Antonio Lang as the opposite forward. Cherokee Parks was an improving center. Jeff Capel took over for Bobby Hurley at point guard, and Chris Collins stepped in for Thomas Hill at shooting guard.

It didn't take long for the nation to see that Mike Krzyzewski had put together another outstanding team. Only this time Grant Hill was definitely the leader. He had deferred to others for three years, but this team was his without a doubt. Duke surprised a lot of people by winning its first ten games. Then came a one-point loss to Wake Forest before the Blue Devils won another five. At 15-1, they were again considered one of the best teams in the country.

Grant, meanwhile, was gaining even more respect. He was leading the Blue Devils in almost every statistical category. He was also leading them in spirit. His winning attitude coupled with a classy demeanor on the court earned him praise wherever the team played.

Then, in mid-February, it was announced that Grant would receive one of the highest honors given a Duke player. Before the game against Temple on February 27, his number 33 would be ceremonially retired. He would be the eighth Duke player to receive this honor. Among the others were Grant's former teammates, Christian Laettner and Bobby Hurley.

"[Playing the game] wasn't difficult," said Grant. "I just tried to play like I always play. I was excited, but just because they were retiring my jersey didn't mean we were going to win the game. We still had to play."

And play they did. Grant had another fine all-around game as the Blue Devils defeated the eighth-ranked Owls, 59-47. Afterward, Temple coach John Chaney couldn't say enough good things about Grant Hill. What he said had been echoed by many others during the course of Grant's career.

"You just don't say 'Shazam' and get a class kid like that," Coach Chaney said. "He's class because his family is class. He's a youngster who reaches back, looks back and knows darn well that he'd like to stick a hand out and help other youngsters."

Duke played out the regular season with a 22-4 record and another ACC regular-season championship. It was apparent now that this was a team with Final Four capability. And this time, Grant Hill was on the first team in every major poll, making him a consensus All-America choice. His career was just about complete.

ANOTHER FINAL FOUR

When the Blue Devils were beaten by Virginia in the second round of the ACC Tournament, their NCAA hopes seemed to fade. But the club came together at the Southeast Regionals, winning the final, 69-60, against a Purdue team that had the top scorer in the country, Glenn "Big Dog" Robinson.

It was a game in which Grant would score just 11 points. But he did a brilliant defensive job on Robinson, holding the Purdue star to just 13 points on 6-for-22 shooting.

Grant was a real high flier as a senior in 1993-1994.
Here he soars high to slam one home in a game
against Clemson. After the season ended he was
named a consensus All-American.

During the 1993-1994 NCAA tournament, Grant got an appreciative hug from Coach K. The coach said that Grant was the best player he had ever coached.

Now Duke was back to the Final Four for the seventh time in nine years. Grant wanted nothing more than to go out a national champion for the third time. In the semifinals, the Blue Devils had to play 14th-ranked Florida. This turned out to be a tough one, as Florida came out hot and took a 39-32 lead into the locker room at the halftime.

Then, in the second half, Grant took over the game. On defense, he checked Florida's Craig Brown, a deadly three-point shooter. Offensively, he set up hoops with his deft passing, and hit a trio of clutch three-pointers himself. When it ended, Duke had a 70-65 victory; Grant had 25 points, 6 rebounds, and 5 assists. The team was in the title game once more.

Once again, Grant was praised for his great, all-around effort. But it was Coach Krzyzewski who gave Grant perhaps the ultimate compliment. Those acquainted with Coach K knew he wouldn't say something like this without a great deal of thought.

"Grant Hill," the coach said, "is the best player I've ever coached, period.

Whether it's ballhandling, defense, shooting, or presence, he does everything at the highest level."

But there was still one more mountain to climb. In the championship game, Duke would be going against Arkansas. The Razorbacks were favored to win their first national title and featured stars Corliss Williamson and Scotty Thurman. But the surprising Blue Devils gave them all they could handle.

It was a close game right from the start. Grant's shots weren't falling in the early going, but he was rebounding like a champ against the tough Razorbacks. At halftime, just a single point separated the two teams as Arkansas led, 34-33. It was still anybody's game.

The second half continued close. It came down to the final minutes. With 1:15 left, Arkansas had a 70-67 lead. Grant got the ball outside and promptly hit a clutch three-pointer to tie the game. But 35 seconds later, Scotty Thurman hit a long three for the Razorbacks to make it 73-70. After that, Arkansas held on for a 76-72 victory and the title.

Although Duke ended up losing the championship, Grant scored 12 points and grabbed 14 rebounds against Arkansas in the NCAA title game. Here Grant battles for the ball with Razorbacks star Corliss Williamson.

Grant had just 12 points in the final, but led both clubs with 14 rebounds and 6 assists. This time, however, it just wasn't enough.

"There's no question that we're disappointed we lost," Grant said. "But we're proud to be able to put ourselves in a position to play for the national championship. I'm not going to hang my head low."

There was no reason for that. In four years, Grant played on Duke teams that had an 18-2 record in NCAA tournament games. They won two national titles and had an overall record of 118-23 during his tenure. In his final season he averaged a team best 17.4 points a game and 6.9 rebounds, second only to center Cherokee Parks. In addition, he led the club in assists with 176 and steals with 64.

He was also the first player in ACC history to amass more than 1,900 points, 700 rebounds, 400 assists, 200 steals, and 100 blocked shots in a career. Besides being a consensus All-American, Grant was also ACC Player of the Year, the MVP of the Southest Regionals, and a member of the All-Final Four team.

So he closed out his college days on top. He graduated with a degree in history and got ready to embark on the next phase of his life—a career as a professional basketball player.

NBA ROOKIE SENSATION

The 1994 National Basketball Association draft was held on June 29. The Milwaukee Bucks had the first pick and tabbed Glenn Robinson, opting for the Big Dog's scoring potential. Dallas, needing someone to run its offense, chose point guard Jason Kidd of California. Picking third, the Detroit Pistons wasted no time in selecting Grant Hill. Many felt that Detroit had gotten the best all-around player available.

In an era when top NBA rookies can command huge contracts, negotiations are never easy. But Grant didn't want to be a holdout or miss the beginning of training camp. When he signed in late September, he was more than satisfied. That's because his first pro contract was an eight-year deal worth some $45 million. It made him the highest-paid athlete in the state of Michigan, and he had still not played his first game as a pro.

"It's pretty weird," Grant admitted, referring to the size of the pact. "But it's the way things are going. I guess, a couple of years from now, a rookie will be coming in here making more than I am."

The Pistons felt their investment was worth it. Billy McKinney, director of player personnel, put it this way: "When we drafted him we felt we were getting the whole package."

Just a few years earlier, the Pistons were the best team in the NBA. Detroit had won

Drafted in the first round by the Detroit Pistons, Grant quickly showed that he could play the rugged NBA game. Here he breaks up a drive to the hoop by the Knicks' Charles Smith (54) and then tries to grab the loose ball.

two straight NBA titles in 1989 and 1990. After that, the team's stars began aging, and the ballclub slowly fell back. The 1993-1994 season was one of transition. The club finished with a 20-62 record, one reason for its high draft pick.

The one star remaining from the Pistons' glory years was shooting guard Joe Dumars. Grant looked forward to playing alongside him and felt things would work out.

"I have my own expectations," he said. "I want to win. I know it's not going to come overnight. It's going to be a gradual process. But if we all stay on the same page, we'll be fine and I think the fans will stay with us."

Grant promised to be the same kind of team player he was at Duke. Donning uniform number 33 once again, he took to the floor with the Pistons and made the transition to the NBA without missing a beat. In fact, he began scoring at a better clip than he ever had at Duke. And he continued to play an all-around, unselfish team game.

Joe Dumars, like Grant, had always been an unselfish player who did what it took to win. Not surprisingly, the rookie and the veteran became fast friends.

"Each guy knows what he has in the other," said Billy McKinney. "Grant sees that Joe is this incredible source of wisdom and support, and Joe sees that Grant is a young player with his head on straight, a player on whom he can have a positive effect. Grant looks at Joe and sees the kind of player he wants to be."

Grant was an outstanding player from the start. Playing small forward, he was doing the same things he had done in his final years at Duke. He was leading the team in scoring, averaging just around the 20-point mark. He was taking down slightly more than 6 rebounds a game and handing out 5 assists per game. Those were outstanding numbers, especially for a rookie.

He was also a crowd pleaser. His quick first step often freed him for spectacular drives to the hoop, which ended, more often than not, in an exciting slam dunk. His jump shot was getting better, and he showed he was ready to bump heads with the toughest players in the league. At 6 feet 8 (203 centimeters), 225 pounds (102 kilograms), he wasn't huge, but his wiry frame reminded many of Chicago Bulls superstar Scottie Pippen.

It was soon apparent that while Grant and Joe Dumars were both bona fide stars, the Pistons needed a lot more to once again become an elite team.

As a professional basketball player, Grant took his responsibilities very seriously. He often volunteered to work with kids at basketball clinics sponsored by the Pistons. Those who weren't chosen to come out on the court with Grant had to be content with taking pictures from the stands.

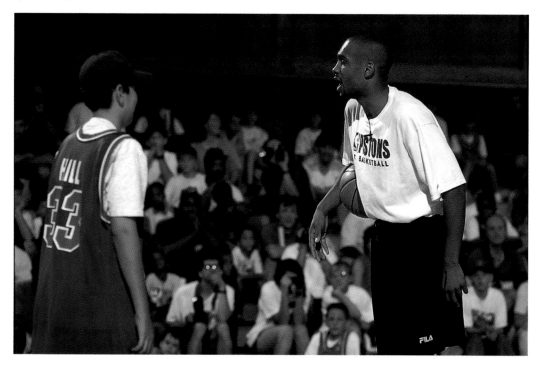

They had some good players and some with potential, but as a team they weren't ready for that next step.

That didn't stop people from praising Grant, who clearly was on his way. Joe Dumars remained one of Grant's biggest boosters. He could see that Grant was just the opposite of many of the other young players coming into the league.

"It's a league of guys who are out of control," Dumars said. "Fringe behavior is being recognized and accepted, sometimes even rewarded. It's probably not a healthy comment that Grant is being recognized for just being a good person, but it's time we get back to that."

There was no trash-talking with Grant, no in-your-face screams after one of his crowd-pleasing dunks. He didn't go out of his way to show anyone up. He just played ball. And at midseason he was rewarded when the fans voted him a starting spot in the annual All-Star Game. Not only was he voted a starter, but he became the first rookie ever to get the most votes of any player.

When told about the voting results, Grant was pleased but humble. "I don't carry myself like an All-Star," he said. "I carry myself as if I'm a rookie trying to make it in the NBA and be as good as I can be. Look at the way I walk. I don't strut; I don't swagger."

Grant started for the East in the All-Star Game and scored 10 points. Though the West won the game, 139-112, he electrified the crowd with a pair of flying slam-dunks off alley-oop passes from Orlando's Penny Hardaway. There was little doubt that he could play with the best.

Grant received more votes than any other starter in the mid-season NBA All-Star Game. Here he goes up for one of two electrifying slam dunks, both coming off passes from Orlando Magic star Penny Hardaway.

During the second half of the season, Grant continued to make many personal appearances to urge youngsters to stay in school. When he gave a speech at a Detroit high school about the value of education, he declined to introduce the new Grant Hill sneaker that day.

"I felt it was inappropriate to say, at the same time, 'Stay in school' and 'Buy my sneaker.'"

All the same, he did have a run of endorsements. Besides sneakers, he also had deals to pitch a number of other products. He was already earning some $5 million a year from endorsements, and one sports marketing expert called him the NBA's most marketable player with the exception of Orlando center Shaquille O'Neal. (That was also before Michael Jordan made his NBA comeback.)

"Hill exudes 'regular guy'," Brian Murphy of the *Sports Marketing Letter* said. "You admire him, but you feel you could talk to him if you met him."

With everything happening so fast, Grant was aware that he might have created too perfect an image.

"I don't want to be any kind of savior," he said. "I'm 22 years old, and I'm going to mess up sometimes. I just don't want that to be a major shock to people."

But there was no messing up the first half of his rookie season, nor in the second half either. He seemed to know just what to say and when to say it. That's because he always thought carefully before he spoke. Nor did he flaunt his newfound wealth like some young athletes do.

Grant has never been afraid to hit the floor in pursuit of a loose ball. Here he scrambles with the Bulls' B.J. Armstrong during heated action between two old rivals, the Pistons and the Bulls.

Late in his rookie season, Grant became a tough, one-on-one player with the game on the line. Here he uses his quick first step to take the ball to the hoop against a single defender.

Grant lived modestly in a three-bedroom condo near the Pistons arena. The only things he had there that might not be found in the average young man's apartment were five arcade video games. Off the court, he was busy organizing a summer camp for kids.

On the court, he was still learning the little nuances of the game. The Pistons were playing the Boston Celtics sometime after the All-Star break. The Celtics had a one-point lead with just six seconds left and the Pistons had the ball. Coach Don Chaney called a timeout.

The coach then diagrammed a play to give Grant the last shot. That, in itself, showed great confidence in the rookie. But Grant knew he was still learning, and as the teams returned to the court he asked the veteran Dumars for any suggestions.

Dumars had watched Grant all year. He saw that in one-on-one situations, Grant liked to hold the ball for a second or two so he could size up the defender before making a move. He also knew what the Celtics would be likely to do.

"They're going to send a guy to double-team you as soon as you touch the ball," Dumars told Grant. "So make your move right away. Don't wait."

Sure enough, Grant got the ball and made a quick move before the second defender could come over. This time, he missed the shot and the Pistons lost. But he had learned something. The veteran Dumars was pleased.

"He'll make the shot a lot more times than he misses it," Dumars said. "And no one will ever have to tell him again how to play in that situation."

Despite Grant's outstanding first NBA season, the Pistons finished last in the Eastern Conference Central Division with a 28-54 record. They didn't make the playoffs. But Grant had a fine year. Though he missed 12 games with assorted injuries, his numbers were still impressive.

Grant led the Pistons in scoring with a 19.9 average, finishing just six points short of averaging 20 a game. He had 445 rebounds, third best on the club, and was second to Dumars with 353 assists. Still a fine defensive player, he led the club with 124 steals and blocked 62 shots. He shot 48 percent from the field and 73 percent from the free-throw line.

After the season ended, it was announced that both Grant and Jason Kidd of Dallas had been chosen Co-Rookies of the Year. Glenn Robinson was third. All three had outstanding first seasons. Grant was pleased to have won, or

shared, the award. But he wouldn't have been too disappointed if he hadn't won. Individual glory has never been part of his makeup. During the off-season he was a sought-after guest on many talk shows. He did public-service spots urging kids to stay in school. He even played the piano on the David Letterman Show.

Young, talented, articulate, intelligent, and wealthy, it would seem that Grant Hill has it all. But he won't rest on his laurels. He has said he wants to become a better player and help the Pistons rebuild and regain their status as one of the NBA's elite teams. He has remained close to his parents, both of whom follow his career closely. And he has always given them credit for the foundation they gave him.

Grant Hill has done things right all his life. But as humble as he usually sounds, he also has a mean competitive streak, the same kind of fire that burns inside all great athletes.

"I don't show it," Grant said, during his rookie year with the Pistons, "but I'm very cocky and very confident underneath. When I show up on the court, I feel I'm the best player out there, and no one can stop me. I want to beat you and embarrass you bad. But I don't want people to know that. It's like a little secret I keep to myself."

Grant dunks over Malik Sealy of the Los Angeles Clippers in a 1995 game in Los Angeles.

GRANT HILL: HIGHLIGHTS

1972   Born on October 5 in Dallas, Texas.

1989   Helps South Lakes High School (Reston, Virginia) win the state championship.

1990   Enters Duke University.

1991   Helps Duke win its first NCAA championship.
Named to Atlantic Coast Conference All-Freshman team.
Named Freshman All-American.

1992   Hill's 18 points and 10 rebounds help Duke win its second NCAA championship.

1993   Wins the Henry Iba Corinthian Award as the nation's top collegiate defensive player.

1994   Becomes the first player in Atlantic Coast Conference history to record more than 1,900 points, 700 rebounds, 400 assists, 200 steals, and 100 blocked shots during his career.
Named All-American.
Named Atlantic Coast Conference Player of the Year.
Named MVP of the Southeast Regionals.
Becomes only the 8th Duke player to be honored by having his number (33) retired.
Taken third in the NBA draft, by the Detroit Pistons.
Selected to play in the NBA All-Star game in his rookie year.

1995   Leads Pistons in scoring (1,394 points; 19.9 average per game) and steals (124).
Becomes the first Pistons player since the 1981-1982 season to score 1,000 points or more in his rookie season.
Named NBA Co-Rookie of the Year, with Jason Kidd of the Dallas Mavericks.
Named to Team USA to represent the United States in the 1996 Olympic Games.

FIND OUT MORE

Duden, Jane and Susan Osberg. *Basketball.* New York: Macmillan, 1991.

Gowdy, David. *Basketball Super Stars.* New York: Putnam, 1994.

Gutman, Bill. *Basketball.* North Bellmore, N.Y.: Marshall Cavendish, 1990.

Hollander, Zander. *National Basketball Association Book of Fantastic Facts, Feats and Super Stats.* Mahwah, N.J.: Troll, 1995.

Rolfe, John. *Grant Hill.* New York: Bantam, 1995.

How to write to Grant Hill:

Grant Hill
c/o Detroit Pistons
The Palace of Auburn Hills
Two Championship Drive
Auburn Hills, MI 48326

INDEX